Saving Montana

Story by John Paolucci

Illustrations by Doris Tomaselli

Special Thanks to (but not limited to)...

Michelle, Ron, Anthony and Charlotte Strollo. Jim Stoner,

Orville Davis & Tamara Alexander.

Denzil McGann, Juan Perez, Greg Scarazzini, Nona Hussey, George Berridge, Laura Ryan,

Dr. Jeremy Frederick (Montana's Vet.), Michelle Malkin, Lonnie Lum, R. Harlan Smith,

Carol Paterno, Jennifer Liebman, Elizabeth Finger Bravard, Shari Finger Fredericks,

Rosalind Kahn, Ed & Gretchen Hueske, Isaac Slager & family, Jim Robinson, Andy and

Cheryl Savage, Don and Bernie McCune, Heather Hill, June Hesler, Christa Myers,

Brenda Heffernan. And for the spiritual gifts I've received from: Lauren Brandstadter,

Joan Mira Gregory, Priscilla Keresey, Don Miguel Ruiz, Patty Edmonds, Eckhart Tolle,

Michael Singer, Sherry White, Dave Hopkins, and—even though her name's

on the cover—I can't thank Doris Tomaselli enough!!

— John —

John, for the opportunity to illustrate Montana's story and for reaffirming

why my heroes have *always* been cowboys.

Frances Bubley, for a peaceful painting spot, long-friendship and lively conversation;

and Geri Brenia, for her friendly visits and colorful suggestions!

— Doris —

ISBN: 978-1-7323600-1-3

Published by Daffodil Press • Daffodil-Press.com
Designed by Empress Creative, Brewster, NY • empresscreative.com
Printed by Service Printers, Duluth, MN • serviceprinters.com

Dedicated to...

To my mother Bridget, the most brilliant, gifted and loving person I've ever known and the inspiration for this book and all my other creative endeavors.

To my dad Umberto (Bert) who is my hero — dedicated, stoic and compassionate beyond words.

And to my sister Anne Marie, who eases the suffering of so many people with her charitable work.

Also to my dearest friend John Castellano, whose passing sent me on the search for happiness that brought Montana and me together.

Not long ago a young man named John
Put cowboy boots and a cowboy hat on.
John had been sad and he thought, "Well, of course,
I know I'd be happy if I rode a horse!"

Not far from his house was a place he'd be able
To meet a nice horse at the local horse stable.
A cowboy named Orville saw John and said, "Howdy!
You'll ride on Montana. He's gentle, not rowdy."

When he saw Montana, John knew right away
He'd have no more sadness by the end of the day.
The big ol' white horse had little brown speckles.
Which Orville called "flecked," but John called them freckles.

When Montana was saddled and ready to ride,
John rubbed his big neck and stood close by his side.
"Mount up!" called out Orville. "And don't take all week!"
Then Montana turned, put his nose to John's cheek.

John had a new friend of whom he was fond,
This white freckled horse with a mane that was blonde.
He saved up his money as all of us should
And rode on Montana whenever he could.

John had a warm feeling whenever he'd ride him
And couldn't help thinking there's magic inside him.
He had a strange thought, and he wasn't sure why,
But inside he knew it, Montana could fly.

One day John arrived and Orville said, "Wait—
You can't ride Montana, with a limp in his gait.
Just pay for your lesson and go wait inside.
I'll saddle a healthier horse you can ride.

"Montana's been stumbling and dragging his feet.
The 'trails' that we ride on are on mostly paved street.
It hurts him to walk pavement day after day.
The owner said, 'Sell him, he'll bring me no pay!' "

"Wait! No Montana?" John wanted his friend!
The sadness he'd lost was now with him again.
John snuck in the stable and looked in the stalls.
Maybe Montana would come if he calls?

So, John made a sound like a long drawn out kiss.
Some white ears perked up to say, "Who now is this?"

There stood our horse in a very small stall.
Oh, this wasn't good for Montana at all!

Orville told John, "Buddy, I am sad too.
Horses are business but here's what we'll do.
We'll ask folks for money, Montana we'll buy.
If he goes to auction, he surely will die."

John felt like an elephant sat on his head.
His whole world would change if Montana were dead.
He tried not to let the tears fall from his eyes.
Just like the old saying that cowboys don't cry.

Although we all know that each life has to end
It's so hard to face when it's family or friends.
John made up his mind this life would not be lost.
He'd rescue Montana, whatever the cost.

In a few days John gave Orville a call.
Who said, "Money's no problem, we've raised it all.
People came out for Montana in force,
But there's no one among them who'll take home a horse.

"He's not like a dog and he's not like a cat;
A horse is a little bit bigger than that!
And what's most important, where he has to be
Must have lots of green pastures where he can run free."

John had an old friend who had moved far away,
His name was Ron and he had this to say:
"Horses cost money, and though I have room
The vet bills and food bills would soon cause my doom!"

John told his friend how his heart was in pain.
Ron owned two horses, no need to explain.
"Build him a stall and then bring him up here.
He'll be *your* horse. You'll have nothing to fear."

10

"I know you love him, but please understand,
A horse is hard work, I bet more than you planned.
You'll have to come often to groom him and see him.
Just say you'll work hard and then let's go and free him."

John gave his word and to Ron he did say,
"I'll build him a stall. I'll start building today!"
So, off to buy lumber John went in a hurry.
He called Orville and said, "Tell Montana don't worry!"

John built a big stall and he built it just right.
To let the sun in, John built a sky light.
With windows that opened and
    fittings of chrome,
It wasn't a stall, it was more like a home.

Ron filled a big feeder with alfalfa hay.
"He won't just eat twice, he'll have food all the day!"
A trailer pulled up and Orville was driving.
John couldn't believe it — Montana's arriving!

When he left the trailer, the horse looked confused.
Then John said, "You're safe here, you won't be abused."
He let out a whinny and ran towards the hay,
Then rolled in the mud and started to play.

Ron's 6 year-old son came to meet their new guest.
Montana loves children so they were both blessed.
Montana and Anthony walked to a stream.
He drank some clear water, just like in a dream.

The two became friends and there's one more surprise,
Ron had one more child, much smaller in size.
Little Charlotte was two and too young, of course,
To be out in the paddock to play with a horse.

John rode Montana through trails in the woods.
Montana was loving his new neighborhood.
Seasons were changing as time quickly passed.
Montana was happy, he was free at last.

When Charlotte grew bigger, a meeting took place.
Our horse fell in love, by the look on his face.
This young girl and he, they made quite a pair.
A tiara she wore in her flowing red hair.

You can't be a princess without a white horse —
A fairy tale rule that must be enforced!
Wherever she traveled, her handsome white steed
Stayed close beside her, so loyal, indeed.

She'd sit on his back without even a saddle.
Montana would grin when he felt her small straddle.
They shared a real bond of true love without fear
And spoke to each other words no one could hear.

John whispered to Charlotte, "Can Montana talk?"
She said, "Yes, he can, and please don't be shocked.
He also has magic, don't let him deceive you,
But tell no one else, 'cause they'll never believe you."

John moved from the city. He moved close to Ron,
Trading tall buildings for acres of lawn.
One day he would want his Montana at home,
But John was afraid that he'd feel so alone.

Both of the children, they loved him quite dearly.
To take him away might hurt them severely.
So John made the choice not to change his address
And take a white horse from his red haired princess!

While out with his friends, John did something tragic.
He told them his thoughts that Montana was magic.
They all laughed at John and said, "Please tell this guy,
That he's lost his mind. He thinks horses can fly!"

Sometimes it is best to keep to yourself
Your hopes and your dreams, and tell no one else.
People get jealous and make fun of you.
Lose faith and your hope and your dreams won't come true!

Not everyone dreams, since we all have fears
That if our dreams fail there'll be lots of tears,
But it's good to dream and important to see,
If dreams don't come true, well, they weren't meant to be.

John started thinking that maybe they're right.
There's no way Montana would ever take flight.
When you say, "No way," well, all hope is gone.
If Montana *can* fly, then it won't be with John.

While gazing at stars, swiftly over John's head
Flew a big streak of white and a small head of red.
"C'mon, Montana, once more 'round the moon,
Then fly away home, Mom and Dad wake up soon!"

Next day John saw Charlotte, and asked her real low,
"How did you your trip 'round the moon last night go?"
Charlotte just smiled, a small kiss she stole.
"Amazing!" she whispered, "but don't tell a soul!"

Montana and Charlotte flew high up above
With magic we all have called faith, hope and love.
When you find your joy, best you don't brag about it,
But share joy with those you see living without it.

What happened to John? Well he wrote this for you,
To tell all about how your dreams can come true.
Thinking good thoughts can change your whole world,
Like it did for the horse and the red headed girl.

Montana had dreams of getting away,
And as you just saw, they came true one day.
Did I ever fly on this horse I love so?
Well, I'll never tell, but maybe you know!

THE END...

You've read the story, now meet the stars! ➡

Meet the real Montana!

Montana meets John's mom when John decides he will rescue Montana.

Montana arrives at his new home!

Montana meets Anthony.

Montana meets Charlotte.

Love is the language of all living things.

Charlotte and Anthony visit Montana,
who now lives with John. (Another dream came true!)

Montana made John's early dream
of being a cowboy come true!